GREAT WAR LITERATURE

GCSE STUDY GUIDE

Written by W Lawrance

on

JOURNEY'S END

A PLAY BY R. C. SHERRIFF

Great War Literature GCSE Study Guide on Journey's End a Play by R C Sherriff
Written by W Lawrance

Published by:
Great War Literature Publishing LLP
Darrington Lodge, Springfield Road, Camberley, Surrey GU15 1AB Great Britain
Web site: www.greatwarliterature.co.uk
E-Mail: enquiries@greatwarliterature.co.uk

Produced in Great Britain

First Published October 2006. Copyright © Wendy Lawrance 2006.
The moral right of the author has been asserted.

ISBN 978-1905378371 (1905378378) Paperback First Edition - October 2006

10 9 8 7 6 5 4 3 2 1

Design and production by Great War Literature Publishing LLP
Typeset in Gill Sans and Trajan Pro

This publication replaces ISBN 978-1905378166 (1905378165).

Great War Literature GCSE Study Guide on

Journey's End

CONTENTS

PREFACE

Great War Literature Study Guides' primary purpose is to provide in-depth analysis of First World War literature for GCSE students.

There are plenty of other study guides available and while these make every effort to help with the analysis of war literature, they do so from a more general overview perspective.

Great War Literature Publishing have taken the positive decision to produce a more detailed and in-depth interpretation of selected works for students. We also actively promote the publication of our works in an electronic format via the Internet to give the broadest possible access.

Our publications can be used in isolation or in collaboration with other study guides. It is our aim to provide assistance with your understanding of First World War literature, not to provide the answers to specific questions. This approach provides the resources that allow the student the freedom to reach their own conclusions and express an independent viewpoint.

Great War Literature Study Guides can include elements such as biographical detail, historical significance, character assessment, synopsis of text, and analysis of poetry and themes.

The structure of Great War Literature Study Guides allows the reader to delve into a required section easily without the need to read from beginning to end. This is especially true of our e-Books.

The Great War Literature Study Guides have been thoroughly researched and are the result of over 25 years of experience of studying this particular genre.

Students must remember that studying literature is not about being right or wrong, it is entirely a matter of opinion. The secret to success is developing the ability to form these opinions and to deliver them succinctly and reinforce them with quotes and clear references from the text.

Great War Literature Study Guides help to extend your knowledge of First World War literature and offer clear definitions and guidance to enhance your studying. Our clear and simple layouts make the guides easy to access and understand.

This new edition of the Great War Literature GCSE Study Guide on Journey's End provides several new chapters and more detail and has been produced in response to requests and suggestions received from schools and examining boards, giving you the most valuable resource available.

JOURNEY'S END
BY R. C. SHERRIFF

INTRODUCTION

This play was originally performed in December 1928 and published the following year. The action takes place in a dugout, in a British trench near St Quentin in France. This is a story of the relationships between five officers between 18th and 21st March 1918, immediately prior to a major battle.

We experience everything from mundane discussions regarding the merits of pineapple over apricots, to the death of one of the officers and the impact this has on those left behind.

There are many moments of humour in the play, particularly at the beginning, which serve to intensify the horrors which the men are experiencing. By introducing humour and detailed personalities into the play, Sherriff demonstrates the human cost of the war which destroyed a generation of young men, the like of which would never be seen again.

SYNOPSIS

ACT ONE

The play opens with Captain Hardy, alone in the dugout, trying to dry his sock, while singing a song to himself. Osborne arrives and the two men share a drink while Hardy finishes dressing. Hardy's regiment is being replaced at the front by Osborne's and the two men discuss what has been happening lately, and the likelihood of a German attack. They talk about the layout and condition of the dugout and trenches and Hardy hands over a list of supplies. The conversation turns to Stanhope - Osborne's company commander. Hardy appears critical of Stanhope's drinking, but Osborne defends him. Although Hardy should really wait and hand over to Stanhope personally, he chooses not to and leaves Osborne to pass on his messages.

The officers' servant - a soldier named Mason - appears and he and Osborne discuss that night's meal. Raleigh arrives: he is a new officer, fresh from England. Osborne welcomes him and, over a drink, it soon becomes clear that Raleigh already knows Stanhope. He explains that they had been at the same school, although Stanhope is three years older. Raleigh's devotion to his old school friend is obvious - in fact it would seem that Raleigh has used some of his family's influence to ensure that he would be assigned to Stanhope's Company. He reveals that Stanhope and his sister share a close friendship, a fact of which Osborne had not previously been aware. Osborne seems concerned that Raleigh might notice some changes in Stanhope and tries to prepare him, as well as explaining some of the routine of the dugout and the trenches.

Raleigh is introduced to Mason, who is worried because a tin which he thought contained pineapple chunks, turns out to be full of apricots and he knows that Stanhope dislikes this particular fruit. Osborne tries to reassure him. Just then Stanhope arrives, together with Second Lieutenant Trotter. Stanhope is angry about the condition of the trenches and orders Mason to bring him some whisky. When he is introduced to Raleigh, Stanhope is shocked to see him and an uneasy atmosphere descends, which Osborne tries his best to cover up.

Raleigh is introduced to Trotter and the men sit down to eat, although Stanhope becomes angry once more when they discover that there is no pepper to go with their soup. While they eat, they discuss their position and their duties for that night. Raleigh is sent on duty with Trotter as it is his first time in the trenches. The man they have relieved - Hibbert - enters the dugout, declines any food and, complaining of a pain in his eye, goes straight to bed. Stanhope seems to think that Hibbert is faking his illness and is unsympathetic. Osborne turns the conversation to Raleigh and Stanhope expresses his surprise that of all the Companies in France, Raleigh should have been sent to his. He shows Osborne a photograph of Raleigh's sister and tells him how concerned he is at how much his personality has changed and how frightened he is.

Stanhope reveals his fear that Raleigh will write to his sister, Madge and reveal the truth about his drinking. Then he realises that he could censor Raleigh's letters and continue to keep his drinking a secret. By now Stanhope is quite drunk and very tired, so Osborne persuades him to sleep for a while, and then retires to bed himself.

ACT TWO

It is the following morning and Stanhope is on duty in the trench, while the other men are eating breakfast in the dugout. They talk about Stanhope, who they think looks unwell, although Raleigh seems embarrassed by the tone of the conversation and is reluctant to criticise his old friend. Sensing Raleigh's discomfort, Osborne changes the subject and they talk about the weather and gardening until Trotter goes to relieve Stanhope. Left by themselves for a short while, Osborne tells Raleigh that he used to play rugby for Harlequins and England, which impresses the younger man. They also discuss the war in general, although when Stanhope returns, Raleigh excuses himself and goes back to his own dugout to finish a letter.

Osborne and Stanhope talk over their immediate tasks, such as repairing the barbed wire, and also the anticipated German attack. Although it is only early in the morning, Stanhope starts drinking. He is very worried about Raleigh's letter and when he reappears with it, ready for posting, Stanhope tells him that he must leave it open on the table so that it can be censored. Raleigh is flustered and initially refuses to show his letter, saying that he will leave it until later. This fuels Stanhope's fears and he wrenches the letter from Raleigh's hand in a violent outburst. Raleigh is shocked by his friend's behaviour and quietly leaves the dugout to go on duty. Osborne is also stunned, but Stanhope turns on him too, before realising that his actions were unnecessarily harsh. He no longer wants to read the letter and throws it down on the table. Osborne offers to glance at it, just to set Stanhope's mind at rest and reads it quietly to himself. When he has finished, he offers to tell Stanhope what Raleigh has said and, although he dreads hearing it, Stanhope agrees. Osborne reads part of Raleigh's letter aloud, which reveals that he feels honoured to be serving with Stanhope; that Stanhope is always tired, but that this is because he is such a good officer who rarely sleeps and is always trying to cheer up the men, and also that the men love him. Raleigh is full of pride that Stanhope is *his* friend. Osborne sticks down the envelope and Stanhope stands, ashamed now that he had doubted Raleigh.

Later that day, Stanhope is issuing instructions to a Sergeant-Major when the Colonel arrives. The Sergeant-Major is excused and then the Colonel reveals that he wants Stanhope to organise a raiding party to be sent across No Man's Land to capture one or two enemy soldiers, in the hope of discovering the strength of the opposition. The Colonel suggests that Osborne should lead the raid and be supported by Raleigh. Stanhope tries to convince the Colonel that Raleigh is too inexperienced, but eventually it is agreed that there is no-one else who could go and the Colonel leaves.

Hibbert appears, having been asleep. He says he feels too unwell to remain at the front. Stanhope tells him that he is suffering from the same complaint himself, but Hibbert persists, saying that he wants to leave the front line and go for medical assistance. Stanhope stops him and says that he will not be allowed to leave: he is not *that* unwell. Hibbert becomes hysterical and goes to collect his belongings, saying that he is going to leave anyway. Stanhope fetches his revolver and, when Hibbert returns and tries to leave the dugout, a heated argument follows during which Hibbert tries to hit Stanhope, who becomes angry and tells Hibbert that, rather than allow him to leave, he would shoot him and make it look like an accident. Hibbert tells him to go ahead - he would rather be shot than have to spend one more moment in the trenches. The two men face each other and eventually, Stanhope replaces his revolver and speaks quietly to Hibbert, telling him how frightened he is. He appeals to Hibbert not to let his comrades down and somehow persuades him to stay, offering to go on duty with him to help calm his nerves.

Osborne comes into the dugout and Stanhope tells him that he is to lead the raid. Stanhope leaves to make arrangements with the Sergeant-Major and a sleepy Trotter appears from his bed. Osborne tells him about the raid and they agree not to discuss the details in front of Raleigh in case he becomes frightened. Osborne is reading *Alice's Adventures in Wonderland* and Trotter seems surprised by his choice of book, although he has never read it himself.

Stanhope returns and collects Hibbert, taking him out into the trench. Osborne and Trotter settle down to some letter writing and Raleigh comes off duty, having been relieved by Stanhope and Hibbert. He has been told about the raid, and is very excited, viewing it as an adventurous opportunity.

ACT THREE

It is the following afternoon and Stanhope is nervously pacing the floor of the dugout, when the Colonel arrives. The two men discuss the plans for the raid. When Osborne and Raleigh come in, the Colonel offers them words of encouragement. Once Osborne and Stanhope are alone, Osborne asks Stanhope to take care of his personal effects, just in case he does not come back from the raid. Stanhope says he will do this, but refuses to acknowledge that Osborne might not return. Finally, Raleigh and Osborne are alone and they go over what will happen during the raid. Then they try to talk about anything else *except* the raid, until eventually the time comes for them to leave. Raleigh suddenly seems nervous, but Osborne calms him down. They leave the dugout, which remains empty, although the noise of the raid can be heard.

When all has gone quiet, Stanhope and the Colonel come into the dugout from the trench. The raid has resulted in the capture of one German soldier who is brought down into the dugout. Stanhope goes back out to talk to the men, while the Colonel interrogates the prisoner. Stanhope returns and the Colonel absent-mindedly asks whether all the men have returned safely, to which Stanhope replies, bitterly, that Osborne and six others have been killed. Raleigh enters the dugout and, after congratulating him, the Colonel leaves. Raleigh sits, dumfounded and in shock, on Osborne's bed. Stanhope has no words of consolation, but simply asks why he must sit there, rather than somewhere else.

Later that evening, Trotter, Stanhope and Hibbert, having dined, sit and tell stories and jokes. This has been a special dinner including chicken and champagne, but Raleigh has chosen to remain on duty in the trench, rather than join them. Hibbert reveals that Raleigh did not want to come to the dinner and preferred to be with the men. This news shakes Stanhope, who becomes angry and orders

Hibbert to go to bed. Once they are alone, Stanhope tells Trotter that he is now second-in-command. Trotter promises not to disappoint Stanhope, and goes out to relieve Raleigh.

When Raleigh enters, Stanhope is angry with him for not attending the dinner and Raleigh makes matters worse by admitting that he has eaten with the men. Stanhope's temper becomes almost uncontrollable and Raleigh is confused, not just by Stanhope's attitude, but also about why they all had a celebratory meal when Osborne had just been killed. Stanhope angrily explains that the drinking and celebration are done to forget, not because he does not care. He dismisses Raleigh.

Very early the next morning, the officers wake up and prepare for the expected attack. Mason is told that he will have to join his platoon in the trench once he has completed his chores. The Sergeant-Major comes down to the dugout to get his instructions. Trotter comes out and calls for Raleigh and Hibbert to join him, before going out into the trench. Raleigh appears and pauses to say goodbye to Stanhope, who barely acknowledges him. Hibbert still has not appeared, so Stanhope calls him again, but when he does come out, he is reluctant to go into the trench. Eventually, Stanhope finds a way around the situation by asking Hibbert to accompany Mason into the trenches. Hibbert can hardly refuse this order and the two men leave. Various messages come down for Stanhope and he gets ready to go up himself. The Sergeant-Major comes down to tell him that Raleigh has been wounded. Stanhope tells him to bring Raleigh down to the dugout and, despite his surprise, the Sergeant-Major obeys and carries Raleigh to Osborne's bed. Raleigh has been badly wounded and Stanhope bathes his head. The two men talk briefly, although Raleigh does not understand the extent of his injuries. Stanhope conceals the truth from him and reassures him that he will be fine. Their friendship is restored as Stanhope briefly takes care of Raleigh in the few minutes before he dies.

A soldier comes down into the dugout and says that Trotter has asked for Stanhope to come up immediately. Stanhope pauses to touch Raleigh's head, before going up into the trench. Just as he does, a shell bursts just outside and the entrance caves in, extinguishing the one remaining candle. All is in darkness and the only sound is of the shells and machine-gun fire.

GLOSSARY OF TERMS

Some of the military language and terminology used in Journey's End can be confusing. We have included below a list of some of the terms or phrases from the play which may require explanation, in alphabetical order.

Billets - Lodging for a soldier, normally in a private home, farm outhouses or public buildings.

Boche - French slang for a German, also adopted by the British.

Dugout - A shelter dug underground. In the First World War, officers at the front essentially lived in these constructions which were sometimes joined together by a series of tunnels.

Funk - Fear or terror.

Lanyard - A cord worn around the waist or neck to secure a gun, knife or whistle.

Lewis Gun - A type of machine gun, used by the British during the First World War.

Log-book - The official record of what has taken place in a particular sector.

MC - Abbreviation for Military Cross. Established in December 1914, this medal was awarded for gallantry to officers, up to the rank of Captain, although it has since been expanded to include other ranks.

Minnies - A German trench mortar, actually named a 'Minenwerfer' which literally translates as 'mine-launcher'.

No Man's Land - Area of land between the front line trenches.

Parapet - The part of the trench which faces No Man's Land, raised to protect the men from enemy fire.

Pavé - French for a type of pavement, usually made of square cobbles on older roads.

Quartermaster-Sergeant - A senior non-commissioned officer who is responsible for supplies.

Sap - A communication trench dug at an angle from the main trench system.

Sentry Post - Position where a man could be positioned to stand guard or observe enemy activity.

Toch-emmas - Army slang for a trench mortar.

Trench Fever - A disease which was quite common in the First World War, causing high fever, headache an back or leg pain. It was transmitted by the lice that infested the men's clothing.

Very Lights - A flare fired from a gun.

Whizzbangs - Slang name used by the British for German artillery. Refers to the noise made by the travelling shell, followed by the explosion.

Wipers - Slang for the Belgian town of Ypres, which saw intense fighting throughout the First World War.

CHARACTERS

STANHOPE

The son of a country vicar, this young captain is the commanding officer of the company of men with whom Journey's End is concerned. Aged approximately twenty-one years, Stanhope has been in the trenches for almost three years, having gone into the army at eighteen. Physically, he is described as tall, thin, and having broad shoulders. The impression created is that he is fastidious about his appearance, having neatly brushed dark hair and a well-cared-for uniform. The description given of Stanhope also refers to the effects of serving in France for three years: although tanned, his face is pale and he appears very tired and drawn.

Even before his first appearance, the conversation between Osborne and Hardy has already made it clear that Stanhope drinks heavily and through the course of the play, we learn that this is done to boost his nerves, which even he appreciates, are shattered. The alcohol also helps him to forget the horrors of everyday trench life and death. This early conversation tells us much more about Stanhope; for example he is fussy about the cleanliness of the trenches. Stanhope likes the trenches and dugouts to be well maintained and with good reason: ammunition stored improperly in wet or damp trenches can go rusty and malfunction; disease can easily be spread amongst the men due to poor sanitation; and he resents the idea of his men, who already have sufficient tasks to keep them occupied, having to spend their time clearing up someone else's mess. To Stanhope, such inefficiency is intolerable. During this same conversation we also discover the high regard in which Stanhope is held. Osborne comments to Hardy that he does not know of anyone who is as good a commander as Stanhope and we learn how much Osborne loves him. Stanhope is obviously an excellent officer, and has been awarded the MC, so his courage is not in doubt to anyone except himself. He is concerned with the welfare of his men: but this concern, together with his experiences and fears have taken their toll on him both physically and mentally. He is a man on the verge of breaking down.

Stanhope appreciates that the war has changed him as a man. When his old friend Raleigh appears in his Company, Stanhope is shocked and he finds it difficult to disguise this. Ever since they were at school together Stanhope has always regarded it as his responsibility to look after Raleigh, particularly as their fathers were old friends. Now his task is harder than ever - taking care of a younger boy at school, and living up to his high expectations is completely different from looking after a junior officer in the front line trenches. He is also aware that Raleigh has always hero-worshiped him, and he is afraid of losing Raleigh's respect once it becomes clear how drastically different he has become. Stanhope would prefer it if Raleigh had been able to remember him as a boy-hood hero, than a broken man, which is how he now perceives himself. In addition he is also concerned that in writing home, Raleigh will betray Stanhope's altered nature and that this might not only shatter his image within his own family, but also with Raleigh's sister Madge, who he obviously loves and with whom he has an understanding. He is keen that Raleigh's sister should be proud of him, and never know of the ways in the which the war has changed him. His outburst when Raleigh refuses to hand over his letter is extreme and shocks his young friend, as well as Osborne, who has clearly never seen Stanhope behave in this way. However, Stanhope soon realises that he has behaved badly and his reaction to the content of Raleigh's letter shows how ashamed he is of his own shortcomings.

Stanhope is conscious of the impression he creates with his men and junior officers and the only person allowed to see him with his guard down is Osborne. Stanhope is very critical of himself but his opinion of his own shortcomings is not reflected by the men in his own Company, who, despite his obvious problems, continue to look up to and respect him. This is not a universally-held opinion, as we have already learned from Hardy that some of the men from outside his company regard Stanhope's behaviour as somewhat freakish or laughable, especially when he is drunk. This may be, however, because it is easier for them to laugh at him than to appreciate that what has happened to him could just as easily happen to them.

Stanhope is a man with a strong sense of duty: while discussing plans with the Sergeant-Major, he suggests that, rather than retreat in the face of the enemy, the company will continue to go forward until they have won the war! This is said half-humourously - Stanhope obviously has no intention of retreating - it would be contrary to his orders, but also he wants to reassure the Sergeant-Major who seems to be worried about the strength of the anticipated attack.

Hibbert's supposed illness demonstrates another side of Stanhope who makes it clear that he will do whatever it takes for the good of his Company. This becomes clear in the episode where Hibbert attempts to evade further participation in the forthcoming attack. Stanhope initially threatens to shoot Hibbert - a fate which would have befallen him anyway, had he deserted. Then, when Hibbert breaks down, Stanhope tells him that he is experiencing exactly the same fears himself. In threatening to shoot Hibbert, we learn that Stanhope places the morale and well-being of the whole company above that of any one man, including himself. If Hibbert had been allowed to carry on behaving as he was, his duties would have suffered and the men might be put at risk as a consequence - a chance which Stanhope is not prepared to take. Stanhope is also aware that, by leaving, Hibbert would be placing an unfair burden on the officers left behind. He also knows that in the long run, it will be better for Hibbert to stay and face the enemy than run and never know if his courage would have failed him at the vital moment. Stanhope reveals his own fears to Hibbert both as a means of shaming the junior officer into staying and also to make him realise that feeling terrified is quite common and is nothing of which to be ashamed. This is an interesting point to note as earlier on, he had been worried that Raleigh's letter home might reveal his own fears and perceived weaknesses. Stanhope, it would seem, is more tolerant and forgiving of other people's defects than of his own. It is also worth noting that Stanhope never reveals Hibbert's actions to anyone, which demonstrates his loyalty to his men.

The news of the planned raid hits Stanhope hard. Initially he offers to take part himself, and then tries to persuade the Colonel that Raleigh is unsuited to the task, which shows that he still feels responsible for his old schoolfriend. Neither of these strategies work, as the Colonel cannot spare Stanhope, and there really is no-one else who can accompany Osborne. He is clearly worried at having to send anyone on this mission, which he feels is not worth risking the lives of his men. When Stanhope and Osborne part, there is an intensity of feeling between them, which is shown in the glances and awkward pauses in their conversation. Stanhope agrees to take care of Osborne's belongings but will not acknowledge the possibility that his friend might not return from the raid. He quite rightly points out that he would be lost without Osborne.

When Osborne is killed, Stanhope is bitter and angry and these are feelings which he takes out on Raleigh, who has returned safely. He acknowledges to Raleigh that in losing Osborne, he has lost his best friend and the one person in whom he could confide - he is unsure of how he will be able to continue without his "Uncle" by his side. He attempts to mask his emotions once again, by drinking and laughing with Trotter and Hibbert, but eventually reveals his true feelings in an angry outburst against Raleigh.

When his old schoolfriend is injured Stanhope reverts to his real personality, trying to spare Raleigh the knowledge of his impending death. This is the real Stanhope, as he was before he became damaged by his experiences in the war. He tenderly cares for Raleigh and looks after him to the very end. His status as hero is restored - both to Raleigh and to himself: he has done his duty.

RALEIGH

Raleigh is the innocent young recruit who arrives, excited at being involved in the war, and particularly at being able to serve under his old schoolboy hero, Stanhope. He is described as a handsome, healthy, but somewhat naive and inexperienced young man.

Upon first arriving, Raleigh is nervous and eager to please, although unsure of how he is supposed to behave. He talks enthusiastically to Osborne of his pre-war friendship with "Dennis" Stanhope. He reveals that he has used his uncle, General Raleigh's, influence to achieve this posting, because he desperately wanted to serve under his old schoolfriend. This is probably partly because Stanhope has always taken care of him and Raleigh hopes this will continue at the front, but also because he simply worships Stanhope and desperately wants to be with him.

Despite Osborne's friendly warnings about the effect that three years fighting has had on Stanhope, Raleigh is still surprised by Stanhope's appearance and his less than enthusiastic welcome. It is as though Raleigh had expected their relationship to be exactly the same as it was when they were at school. Upon first witnessing Stanhope's drunkenness, Raleigh appears shocked and seems to prefer not to be in company with his old friend.

Stanhope's reaction to his letter also comes as a blow to Raleigh. He had not anticipated that his letter would need to be censored, presumably because he feels that Stanhope should trust him and he is embarrassed by the prospect of Stanhope reading the contents of his letter. Stanhope misreads Raleigh's reluctance and reacts violently towards him. Raleigh begins to understand the effects of the war on Stanhope, but is still confused, and disappointed by his friend's reaction. In this letter, however, he reveals nothing of Stanhope's changed nature, but remains loyal himself, pointing out instead how hardworking and tireless Stanhope is and that he is an excellent and well-respected officer. He finishes by telling his family of his pride in the knowledge that Stanhope is his friend.

On hearing that he is to help lead the raiding party, Raleigh is nervously enthusiastic. As the hour approaches, his nerves begin to dominate his enthusiasm and it is Osborne who comforts him. His youth and inexperience are revealed in this scene as he talks nervously to Osborne, trying not to dwell on the raid, refusing to have rum in his coffee and pointing out that he has never smoked a cigar before. This also emphasises the difference in age between the two men, with Raleigh seeming, more than ever, like the schoolboy while Osborne is the wise, kind and inspiring "school teacher".

After the raid, when Osborne is dead, Raleigh is clearly in shock and can barely stand up as he speaks to the Colonel. This new experience has made him understand the horror of the war - something which Stanhope had obviously wanted to spare him for as long as possible. Raleigh slowly comes to realise how much Osborne had meant to Stanhope. He feels left out of Stanhope's thoughts and doesn't understand his reactions. He wants to be involved and to help Stanhope, but cannot because his friend will not communicate with him. Raleigh would prefer to talk about his feelings, both for Osborne and for Stanhope, but Stanhope rejects this overture, angrily pushing Raleigh away.

There is an awkwardness between Raleigh and Stanhope because Raleigh had assumed that by being with Stanhope, everything would be as it was at school. He has also failed to understand that the war has changed Stanhope to such an extent - he remembers his friend as a young dashing officer, keen to join the fight, and barely recognises the man he has become. Stanhope, on the other hand, resents Raleigh's presence as a reminder of his old life and the person he once was. In addition, Stanhope has formed new friendships now, especially with Osborne, who he looks up to and respects. These are not the sort of feelings he can have for Raleigh whose innocence represents everything he has lost.

Ultimately, the only time that Raleigh is able to recapture the old Stanhope, is on his death-bed, as we get a glimpse of what their relationship once was. His hero looks after him and ensures that he feels safe, comfortable and unafraid.

OSBORNE

While significantly older than Stanhope, Osborne is junior in rank. Married, with two children, he is physically tough and rugged - the opposite of his personality which is level-headed, friendly and trusting. His feelings for his family are clear when he tells Stanhope that he spent the whole of his last leave at home with them, not even going to see any shows. He describes with great warmth the peaceful evenings spent with his wife and playing at soldiers with his two sons. His choice of reading material is interesting: *Alice's Adventures in Wonderland* presumably reminds him of happier times at home. However, once he is back at the front, the Company become his family.

Osborne is very protective of Stanhope, trying to help him wherever possible. Their relationship is not based on hero-worship: Osborne knows and appreciates Stanhope's faults but his respect for his senior officer is borne out of years of experience and time spent with Stanhope at the front. Osborne realises that being in command brings with it heavy responsibilities and he knows that these have taken their toll on Stanhope; despite this, however, Stanhope has remained an excellent and diligent officer, and it is this which earns him Osborne's love and respect. He defends Stanhope's actions to Raleigh and especially Hardy, showing his loyalty to his commanding officer.

Osborne is very kind to Raleigh, who is nervous when he first arrives. He tries to warn Raleigh that Stanhope has changed and also attempts to deflect Raleigh's hero-worship by pointing out that he had played rugby for Harlequins and England. This is not done in a boastful manner, but more as a means of diverting Raleigh's attention from Stanhope, who he knows will be troubled by Raleigh's presence. He is not a vain man which he demonstrates when Hardy suggests that he would make a better Commanding Officer than Stanhope - a suggestion which he adamantly refutes.

As a former school master, Osborne is used to looking after boys, and sees his position in the dugout as an extension of this role, to the point where he is nicknamed "Uncle". He is always on hand with sensible advice and words of wisdom and is keen to avoid conflict within the dugout. It is always Osborne who helps Stanhope, especially when he is drunk, or over-tired. His first concern is to protect his Commanding Officer from the prying eyes and judgement of others, but also from the most destructive influence in Stanhope's life - himself.

Osborne is very diplomatic: for example, his method of getting Mason to wash the dish-cloth is to ask his wife to send him out some soap powder and then suggest to Mason that he might like to try using it. Also when there is obviously a problem with Hibbert, Osborne deflects Trotter's enquiries and changes the subject.

His silences upon being told that he is to lead the raid, and his desire not to talk about it beforehand, demonstrate that he is wary of being sent on this mission. He is an officer of some experience and has been on raids before, but now he seems to have a sense of his own mortality as he gives his belongings to Stanhope for safe-keeping, to be returned to his wife should he not survive. He naturally overcomes his own nerves, at least for appearance's sake, and calms the nerves of Raleigh, who has never experienced anything like this before and, as the hour approaches, becomes more and more nervous. Osborne's attitude towards the men is always caring and considerate and although he is an officer of some standing, he has not yet become war-weary, like Stanhope. He has a sensible yet realistic perspective of the war.

Osborne's death signifies a change for this small group of officers. Raleigh, who was with him at the time, feels guilty and disturbed by

Osborne's death, while Stanhope has lost the one fellow officer he knew he could trust implicitly. Even if the attack had not happened the next morning, one senses that this Company of men would never have been quite the same again.

TROTTER

Trotter is obviously not in the best physical shape - he is rotund and red-faced. He is also middle-aged with a bursting tunic - the result, no doubt, of too much indulgence in his favourite interest - the consumption of food. He is married and his letters to his wife and descriptions of his home life, such as his garden, serve to remind us that all of these men have something to live for, and so much to lose.

He is a friendly, tolerant character, who is supportive of his fellow officers and loyal to Stanhope. He is also concerned about Stanhope's drinking and health, although he does not have the same close relationship as his Commanding Officer shares with Osborne. Unlike the other officers, Trotter has been promoted through the ranks and, presumably, does not have the same public school background as them, which is demonstrated by the fact that his language is more colloquial than theirs. Outwardly, Trotter appears to be very unemotional, but the impression is given that this is only on the surface and that Trotter's feelings go much deeper than it would seem. In fact, when Stanhope says that he envies Trotter for being able to maintain a sense of normality, Trotter makes it clear that this is most definitely not the case. He doesn't like to talk about how he feels, using humour to overcome difficult circumstances, and therefore he falsely creates the impression that he doesn't feel anything.

Stanhope and Osborne, while liking Trotter, feel that he lacks imagination: they believe that they look more deeply at life, while he merely observes what is on the surface. This demonstrates one of the perceived differences between their classes. They have drive and ambition, while Trotter is happy with his lot in life. This is reinforced later on, when he points out that he has never owned a car, but that he and his wife used to walk everywhere together, but he does not seem to resent the fact that others have more than him.

Many critics describe Trotter as an artificial character - somewhat unnecessary to the plot. This does him a grave injustice as his importance lies in the subtleties of what he says: his reactions demonstrate the common feeling. So, for example, he's worried about the raid - even though he is not involved - but he knows that it is useless to argue, as the orders will not be revoked, no matter how pointless and costly the raid might be. He knows that nothing he can do will change the course of the war, but equally he does not see why he should have to suffer more discomfort than is absolutely necessary. Much of the humour in the play emanates from Trotter and centres on his love of food. Not only does he joke about things, but the others make fun of him, although this is never done offensively, but in friendship.

After Osborne's death, Trotter becomes Stanhope's second-in-command, but this brief relationship is more formal than Stanhope and Osborne's had been. Trotter feels honoured by the promotion and promises not to let Stanhope down. Even on the final morning, immediately before the attack, Trotter appears cheerful - he sings songs while in his dugout which helps to relieve the feeling of tension and probably also serves to take his own mind off what might lie ahead.

HIBBERT

Hibbert is a young, slightly obscure man with a pale face - reminiscent of a weasel - both in appearance and manner.

First impressions of Hibbert are not good. He complains of feeling unwell almost continuously and craves escape from the trenches.

Hibbert doesn't initially interact with his fellow-officers, although he knows them all well, preferring to sleep and keep his own company whenever he is not on duty, although one gets the impression that he does this to support his argument that he is unwell.

During his quarrel with Stanhope, it becomes clear that Hibbert is terrified of going back into the trenches and is persuaded to stay only by Stanhope first threatening and then sympathising with him. This exchange shows Hibbert in an unfavourable light and although he agrees to stay, he then becomes concerned that Stanhope might tell the others of his cowardice. This confirms that Stanhope had been right in his assumption that Hibbert was faking his illness, and also shows that Hibbert is a shallow man whose sole concerns are his own welfare and reputation.

This bad impression is exacerbated by his reaction to Osborne's death. Whereas for Trotter and Stanhope, the meal and light conversation are a means to forget, Hibbert uses this opportunity to show off his lewd postcards and boast of his exploits with women - he simply wants to enjoy himself. He also gossips about Raleigh which shows he does not share the common sense of loyalty, which he seems to expect of others. Stanhope's distaste for Hibbert is obvious throughout the play, but really comes out in this scene.

When the time comes to go back into the trenches, he is again hesitant and fearful. In fact he has to be called several times before appearing on the morning of the final attack. He seems unwilling to go up into the trenches, wasting a great deal of time and making excuses, until Stanhope tells him to accompany Mason. This is Stanhope's way of shaming Hibbert into doing his duty - if Mason can do it, so can he. Although this works and Hibbert goes, he hesitates again and, unlike all the others, does not say anything to Stanhope.

MASON

Mason is essentially a servant and his general responsibility is to take care of the officers to whom he is assigned. He cooks their meals and clears up after them. This does not, however, mean that he escapes the fighting - he must also take part in any battles in which his company are involved.

Although we are told little about Mason's appearance or personality, we can conclude that he is hard-working, loyal and caring. He never questions his orders, and is keen to please. For example, prior to the final battle, he makes sandwiches for the officers, before going up into the trenches. Mason is often the butt of light-hearted jokes about food and cooking, but this is done without malice.

When Stanhope suggests that Hibbert and Mason go up into the trench together, Mason appears grateful, which may demonstrate his own nervousness. This could, however, be interpreted as showing Mason's understanding of the real situation surrounding Hibbert and his desire to be useful to Stanhope.

The role of Mason's character in the play is to provide humourous respite in the building tension, his interactions with Trotter being particularly amusing. He also serves to remind us that, for the officers in the dugout, in spite of their surroundings and horrific experiences, ordinary activities still go on. The men must eat, and the discussion of what they are eating and how it has been cooked provides a useful diversion from the war, and in many cases, helps to enhance the human qualities of the play.

HARDY

Hardy is a Captain, who commands the company from whom Stanhope's men are taking over. It would seem that he has been at the front for some time, as nothing really seems to surprise him. His role in the play is to set the scene. His conversation with Osborne serves the purpose of explaining the anticipated attack, and Stanhope's personality, as well as some of the boredom and routine of trench-life.

Hardy is a humourous, philosophical character, who has a light-hearted outlook on almost everything, including the general hardships of the war, although this might be more obvious as he is being relieved and going behind the lines - whether he would be as amused if he were the one coming into the trenches is another matter.

This initial scene involving Hardy helps to set the tone for the rest of the play, and helps the reader or audience appreciate that this black humour was an important aspect of life in the trenches. During this scene, as well as learning about the still absent Stanhope, we also learn a great deal about Osborne and how well-respected he is amongst the other men - even those not in his own Company.

The ruins of St Quentin.
Photo Credit: Photo's of the Great War

Entrance to St Quentin canal tunnel under the ridge at Bellicourt, on the Hindenburg Line.
Photo Credit: Photo's of the Great War

HISTORICAL SIGNIFICANCE

The historical setting of the play is significant and accurate. The play starts on March 18th 1918 which was three days before the Germans launched "Operation Michael" at St Quentin.

This was Germany's attempt to end the war before the Americans could arrive in any great number and therefore tip the balance of power in favour of the Allies. Germany, like most of the countries involved in the First World War, was running out of men of military age and the success of this attack was therefore vital.

General Erich Ludendorff declared that the object of this attack must be a resounding victory over the British and the selection of the place for the proposed attack was therefore, of great importance. Immediately in front of the St Quentin trenches was the old Somme battlefield. This was difficult terrain which consisted of water-logged shell-holes and abandoned trenches. Ludendorff thought that, both tactically and psychologically, this was the ideal place to strike. The intention was that, by use of specialist storm troops, the German army would punch a hole in the British front line, and force a retreat towards the coast. However, Ludendorff had no fixed idea as to what would follow this initial strike.

The first days of this battle were extremely bloody and losses on both sides were heavy. It would not be surprising, therefore, if all the characters in *Journey's End* died, since the bombardment and subsequent attack resulted in many British deaths. As a result of these initial losses and the speed of the German advance, the Allied armies became separated which resulted in arguments between Haig (Commander in Chief of the British Army) and Pétain (his equivalent in the French force). At a hastily convened meeting the Allies decided to have one Supreme Commander, which it was decided should be Marshal Ferdinand Foch. This was a significant step and enabled the Allies to fight in a more co-ordinated fashion, with reserves and weaponry being better deployed.

Germany failed to exploit her initial successes and rather than continuing with the plan of a single-pronged attack, her forces became divided. In addition, the selection of the old Somme battleground now seemed unwise as it proved to be difficult terrain for an attacking army to advance over. In addition, the Germans had advanced much further than their lines of supply could support, so by 5th April the German High Command were forced to admit that Operation Michael had achieved as much as could be expected, and further attacks in this area were abandoned.

Before long, American troops began to arrive and this had a great demoralising effect on the German army. Attacks continued at other points on the front and it would take many more months, and many many more deaths before the war was over.

Field Marshal
Sir Douglas Haig

General
Henri-Philippe Pétain

Marshal
Ferdinand Foch

Photo Credits: Photo's of the Great War

RANKS IN THE BRITISH ARMY

Some students find the named ranks and their responsibilities difficult to interpret. The following provides a very brief outline of the role of each of the ranks involved in *Journey's End*.

COLONEL

The most senior officer involved in the play, the Colonel is, in all probability, in charge of a battalion of over 1000 men, divided into four companies. The company involved in Journey's End is 'C' Company. During the course of the war, with the influx of the New Armies and the number of casualties the quantity of men in a battalion varied widely.

CAPTAIN

This rank belongs to the characters of both Stanhope and Hardy. These men are both in charge of companies of approximately 230 men. They are responsible for the maintenance of their area of trench, as well as the morale and physical well-being of the men under their command. It is their duty to ensure that the men are in a fit state to undertake whatever tasks they must perform - whether that involves fighting in battle or 'fatigues' (manual labour, such as clearing roads, digging trenches etc.)

LIEUTENANTS AND SECOND LIEUTENANTS

These ranks apply to all the other officers in the play. It may fairly be assumed that Osborne is superior in rank to Trotter, Hibbert and Raleigh, as he is Stanhope's second-in-command, so he probably holds the rank of Lieutenant, while the others are Second-Lieutenants. Their responsibilities were essentially to help their captain in maintaining the day-to-day running of the company. In addition, each of these men would have been responsible for a Platoon within the company, consisting of approximately 50 men each.

COMPANY SERGEANT-MAJOR

This rank is held by the most senior non-commissioned officer in a company. A commissioned officer being one who has been charged, or 'commissioned' into a specific position. The CSM is, generally speaking, responsible for standards and discipline amongst the lower ranks. Beneath him there would be other sergeants and the men. In times of battle the CSM is responsible for seeing to the safe removal of the wounded and dealing with prisoners

OTHER RANKS

These include Sergeants, Corporals, Lance Corporals and Privates. The only named 'other rank' in the play is Mason, the officer's servant, who in this role would be the only soldier, other than the officers, to spend much time in the dugout.

R C SHERRIFF - BIOGRAPHICAL DETAIL

Robert Cedric Sherriff was born on 6th June 1896 in Kingston-upon-Thames, although some sources say he was born in adjacent Hampton Wick. He was educated at Kingston Grammar School and then New College, Oxford. He worked in his father's insurance company until the outbreak of the First World War.

In August 1914, Sherriff attempted to obtain a commission into the British Army. He later related the story of his interview with an adjutant, presumably with some irony. Sherriff, it would seem, was informed that he would probably not be a suitable candidate for a commission as he had not attended a public school. Somewhat mystified by this, he explained that his school was a good one and had been founded by Queen Elizabeth I in 1567. However, the adjutant remained unimpressed - pointing out that his orders were only to accept applications from men who had attended recognised public schools.

The stupidity of this ruling must have had a bearing on Sherriff, who despite his supposedly "poor" education was no less qualified to serve as an officer than his public school colleagues.

Sherriff went on to serve as a captain in the East Surrey Regiment, arriving in France on 28th September 1916. After the war, he rejoined his father's company, where he remained for the next ten years.

He had always been interested in amateur theatricals and wrote plays for performance by members of the Kingston Rowing Club to raise money for a new boat. This led him to write *Journey's End*, based on his experiences in the war. The play was first performed one Sunday evening in December 1928 and went on to become a huge success.

This achievement enabled Sherriff to become a full-time writer and he went on to write many more plays and several screen plays for films including *Goodbye Mr Chips*, *The Four Feathers* and *The Dam Busters*. He also published his autobiography, *No Leading Lady*, in 1968.

He lived in Esher, Surrey until his death on 13th November 1975. He left his house, named Rosebriars to Elmbridge Borough Council for social and cultural purposes. The capital raised from the sale of this house established the R C Sherriff Rosebriars Trust which still exists today to promote the arts in the Borough of Elmbridge.

THEMES

FUTILITY AND WASTE

Journey's End is now generally recognised as an anti-war play, although some historians doubt that this was Sherriff's original intention. Some confusion, it would seem, arose from a difference of opinion between Sherriff and the play's original producer. Sherriff's intention was, rather, to portray the pride which the men felt in each other and the comradeships which developed in such difficult circumstances. In doing so, he also demonstrates the human cost of the war, in that the men seem to be required to give their lives - and even those who survived would never be the same again - for no reason. Death is indiscriminate, taking those who least deserve to fall, and these deaths are seen to serve little or no purpose. The men are generally portrayed as worthy people who have accepted their presence in the war as something they had to do - a necessary evil. Although the men, especially Stanhope, may question the value of activities such as the raid, none of them speak out against the war itself, despite the fact that it costs them all dearly.

These themes are best demonstrated immediately before and after the raid, led by Osborne and Raleigh. The purpose of this raid is to capture some German soldiers to find out where the anticipated attack is likely to take place, and the strength and nature of the opposing army. The colonel points out, somewhat optimistically, that the success of this raid may constitute an early end to the war. However, the discovery of the type of opposition you are facing is unlikely to affect the outcome of a battle, if you have nothing more to throw at it yourself. Therefore, it would seem that the colonel is seeking to justify the raid, when in fact, as Stanhope suggests, there can be no justification for such a waste of lives. The raiding party manages to capture a young German soldier, whose limited information is greeted with disproportionate pleasure by the Colonel. He appears to feel that the raid has accomplished its aims. The details given by the captured German soldier, however, seem insignificant compared with the loss of life necessitated during his seizure.

The deaths of Osborne and six of the men accompanying him, is a great price for this Company to pay. For Osborne - surely the most likeable character in the play - to have died at all is lamentable, but to have died for so little and in such circumstances is tragic - a point which Stanhope grasps, and which makes him bitter and angry towards the Colonel. Stanhope appreciates that it is really Osborne who holds the Company together, not himself, because he has come to rely so heavily on Osborne as the war has progressed. Nothing has really been gained by these deaths and Sherriff uses Osborne's death in particular to reinforce the idea of this war's destruction of the best men of his generation.

Throughout the play, however, Sherriff also shows that death is not the only means of wasting a life: Stanhope has virtually suffered a nervous breakdown, changing from the self-assured, sportsman and hero of Raleigh's description, to a confused and moody wreck, who doubts his own abilities and constantly looks to Osborne for reassurance. Raleigh, on the other hand, loses his innocence: he learns a difficult lesson as he comes to realise that Stanhope is not the man he once knew and that the war has changed his friend forever. Ultimately Raleigh also loses his life - within a few minutes of his first experience of battle - but not before he has witnessed the physical and emotional damage that the war can bring about. Had either Stanhope or Raleigh lived, it is unlikely that they would ever have fully recovered from their experiences. Stanhope actually realises this already, as he shows in his conversation with Osborne, when he says that if he survives he will go away by himself for a long time, to recover his health, before trying to face Madge again.

Another example of futility comes in a seemingly strange conversation when Osborne and Stanhope discuss the fate of worms. The two men agree that worms probably have no idea in which direction they are travelling and how rotten and confusing this must be for them. This minor conversation could be interpreted as a reference to the equal pointlessness of the men's existence - they also have very little idea of where they are going, or why, and yet as Osborne says - with more than an air of sarcasm, this pointlessness and confusion is dreaded by the worms more than anything else. He is implying that there are worse situations to be in than wasting your time drifting aimlessly; being killed, without ever really understanding the reason, for example, could as easily befall the worm or the soldier.

The choice of *Alice's Adventures in Wonderland* as reading material for Osborne is also interesting. Osborne quotes from the book to Trotter, who finds the passage pointless and playfully mocks Osborne for reading a children's book. Of course, Osborne's point is that it *is* pointless - not just the passage quoted, but everything - this story represents how little meaning there is in the men's lives, and how nonsensical the whole war has become. For most of the men, especially those like Stanhope and Raleigh, the point of joining up was for the "adventure" and to do their duty, not to sit around in trenches, waiting to be blown up, or being sent on pointless raids into No Man's Land.

BOREDOM AND TENSION

Most of the play is spent waiting for something to happen, whether it is a raid, the impending attack or the serving of a meal. Hardy tells us right at the beginning of the play that the men can sit in boredom for hours and hours and then, suddenly, without warning, something unexpected will happen.

The tension created by this sense of anticipation provokes different responses in each of the characters. Hibbert, for example, dreads going up into the trenches and longs for the waiting to continue - anything as long as he doesn't have to face the realities of his situation. He spends most of his time asleep in his dugout, not mixing with the other men. By avoiding them he also avoids the issue of what might be about to happen, because he is not there to hear it being discussed. His supposed illness is his means of trying to escape, although it also tells us a lot about his personality. Hibbert's reaction is a form of denial: by pretending to be unwell and avoiding the others, he is trying to appear as though the war has not really affected him psychologically, but that it has made him physically ill. The truth, of course, is revealed during his argument with Stanhope, when he is forced to confess his real feelings.

Stanhope on the other hand, 'copes' by keeping busy, not sleeping and drinking himself into oblivion. By doing this he not only takes his mind off the reality of his life, but also helps to pass the time doing anything other than thinking - a necessity of his position which has become abhorrent to him. In addition to not thinking about his current situation any more than is absolutely necessary, Stanhope also seems to have been avoiding thoughts of his past. Raleigh's arrival necessities a resurgence of these memories and, for the first time, he tells Osborne about his feelings for Madge. Osborne is Stanhope's closest friend and yet he has never spoken of Raleigh's sister before. He has obviously found it necessary to block out his memories of the past, in order to maintain a semblance of a focus on the present. Remembering these things only seems to add to his tensions which become more obvious as the raid approaches. He paces the floor, glances about anxiously, checks his watch repeatedly - showing that the strain of waiting is making him even more nervous than normal. He also busies himself with the last-minute preparations so as to avoid thinking about what might happen.

Osborne tries to help wherever he can and relieves his boredom by reading *Alice's Adventures in Wonderland*. He is a great observer of everything which is going on around him. He talks to the others, helping to relieve their nerves, especially Raleigh, who has no idea what to expect. Probably the most tense moment in the play is the scene between Raleigh and Osborne immediately prior to the raid. Once they have finalised their plans, Osborne suggests that they try to forget about the raid for the final few minutes before it commences. It takes several attempts and a quotation from *Alice in Wonderland* before Osborne succeeds in changing the subject. The tension actually seems to increase as they discuss their homes and talk of Osborne visiting Raleigh after the war. There is an unspoken fear that, in all probability, one or other of these men may not return and they make plans for the future to cover this up.

Trotter eats, thinks about eating, or talks about eating, and writes to his wife of mundane, everyday matters, such as his garden and the lice which have infested his clothing. He has created a chart of circles to count down the hours until they can be relieved and go back down the line. Trotter uses humour to overcome these difficult situations, although there is always the underlying hint that he feels much more than he expresses.

Only Raleigh, the new recruit is, as yet, unaffected by the boredom, as he is keen to impress the others, so he pays attention and makes sure that he is doing his duty to the best of his ability. Although he is unaware of what lies ahead in the raid, the tension of waiting to go out into No Man's Land is obvious and his nerves start to get the better of his excitement, although Osborne helps to calm him down. Once Osborne has been killed, Raleigh's sense of adventure and excited anticipation disappear, to be replaced by the same sense of sorrow and foreboding as the rest of the men.

In reality these feelings of boredom and tension were common among serving soldiers in the First World War. Their feelings of terror during battles could be said to have been increased by the fact that so much of their time was spent doing mundane and repetitive tasks, waiting for something to happen. It was all or nothing.

SCHOOLDAYS AND HEROES

There is a strong comparison drawn between life in the trenches and at a "public" school. Not only were Raleigh and Stanhope at the same school, but Osborne, in private life, was a school master. At the time of the First World War, the title "public" school was given to fee-paying establishments, of which many were also boarding schools. Therefore, there is an atmosphere of the school dormitory in the dugout, and a definite sense of hierarchy, with certain officers taking precedence over others, and the emphasis being on experience and seniority. For instance, right at the beginning of the play, Hardy points out the best bed in the dugout to Osborne, telling him that the others do not have bottoms to them. As the senior officer of his Company, Hardy has the best bed, while the other officers have to make do with whatever is left. Stanhope, on the other hand, designates the best bed to Osborne, preferring to sleep nearer to the table, so he can work during the night without disturbing anyone else.

Stanhope is given the air of the "head boy", looking after those younger or less experienced than himself, especially the new boy - Raleigh. Although we are led to believe that Stanhope was happy to wear this mantle while at school, it does not sit well with him now. He says that he used to enjoy looking after Raleigh and the influence that he was able to exert over the younger boy, but now he feels uncomfortable at having so much additional responsibility thrust upon him. He also wishes that he could have been spared the indignity of having Raleigh witness what has become of him - he feels that his hero's crown has slipped and does not want to crush Raleigh's image of him. It would seem that Stanhope took his status at school quite seriously. Raleigh recalls Stanhope's attitude towards smoking and drinking when they were at school, which goes to show how much of an impact the war has had, being as Stanhope now drinks so much himself.

Raleigh, on the other hand, as the new boy is eager to please and do well, just as he probably would have been at school. His personality makes him keen to learn, although he is as yet unsure of the rules and protocols which exist in the trenches. At school, Raleigh had worshipped Stanhope and looked up to him as someone worthy of respect, finding it impossible to see a fault in Stanhope's personality. He is keen that this relationship should continue in the trenches and hopes that Stanhope will not object to his presence. Osborne has to try and warn Raleigh about his hero's altered personality and the effect that the war has had on him. Raleigh's hopes for a resumption of his friendship with Stanhope may be because he assumes that the continuation of certain aspects of his life at home will give him an increased sense of security - reminding him, perhaps, of happier days at school.

Osborne, with his worldly experience is the voice of reason and sanity - the housemaster. He offers sensible advice and provides a caring, responsible figure for the others to turn to. As a former school-master, he is perfectly suited to this role as he understands the problems of boys who find themselves away from home. It must be remembered that Stanhope, when he first went out to the front, and Raleigh, when he arrives, are extremely young - and have arrived straight from school. Osborne's presence must be very welcome and reassuring to both of them. A good example of this relationship is when Stanhope asks Osborne to tuck him up in bed - this shows not only Stanhope's youth, but also Osborne's caring and understanding nature.

We also have Mason, who in the role of servant, helps recreate the public school hierarchy. The officers chastise him for not bringing any pepper to go with their soup, and he worries (quite disproportionately) about the prospect of having to serve apricots instead of the desired pineapple. His worries serve to remind us of his 'inferior' status, when compared to the officers.

Trotter is the only one of the officers who, it would seem, did not attend a public school. This is demonstrated by his tone and language, which is more colloquial than the others. Also, we learn that he has risen from the ranks, which would have been the only course open to him at the beginning of the war. This is interesting, as it means that rather than being commissioned as an officer from the very beginning, he has worked his way up, by being good at what he does. The difference in his education could provide a reason why Trotter keeps his views to himself most of the time: although they are all friendly enough, he possibly does not feel that he really fits in with the others.

Stanhope's treatment of Hibbert, when the latter tries to evade his duties, is reminiscent of schooldays. Although he is obviously more extreme in his language and the nature of his threats, one can easily imagine Stanhope berating Hibbert for refusing to turn out for a rugby match, or not doing his best in the last game of cricket. Hibbert is, in fact, the only member of the company who does not show Stanhope very much respect, but then we are not told what his background is, so we do not know whether he is a public schoolboy. His language ties in with most of the other officers, but his behaviour is not so honourable as theirs. His role in the play demonstrates a less appealing type of personality whose position at school would probably have been the boy who cheated in his exams.

There are many references to rugby and cricket which help reinforce this "public schoolboy" image of England as it was before the First World War and most of the men attempt to maintain these old school standards throughout: by respecting their superiors, not questioning their orders and being loyal to one another.

FAMILY

Whilst these men are all very different, in terms of background, experience and personality, they have become like a family and have adopted roles within that family. There is a powerful sense of belonging and of loyalty which most of the men exhibit throughout the play and those who do not are chastised for their attitude.

Osborne, the oldest and wisest, is nicknamed "Uncle" - a well deserved and appropriate epithet since he is always on hand with sensible advice, is supremely loyal and kind, yet not overbearing or interfering. His maturity and experience, both before and during the war, help him to understand the others. Osborne's adoption of this nickname enhances this family theme and encourages the audience or reader to look for further examples of it.

Stanhope, despite his youth, is a father-figure to his men - which was not an uncommon role for company commanders in the First World War. He has to take all the tough decisions and deal with the consequences both of his own and others' actions. This responsibility weighs heavily on one so young, and has taken its toll on Stanhope, who is on the verge of a nervous breakdown relying heavily on the senior members of his "family" for support. Their loyalty and respect for him are obvious - and well deserved. Despite his many faults, he always puts them first.

Raleigh is the equivalent of the youngest son in the family - looking to his elders for advice and approval. He worships Stanhope blindly and his attachment to his friend is clear: when writing to his family at home, he makes no mention of Stanhope's problems with alcohol or his changed temperament - putting any noticeable changes in Stanhope's personality down to tiredness and overwork. Like many younger sons, he doesn't yet have a fixed idea of what his future holds and is content, for the time being, at least, to follow in the footsteps of those who have preceded him.

The role of older brother goes to Trotter, who is quiet, considerate and has a good sense of humour which sees the family through difficult times. He keeps his own counsel and doesn't interfere but is willing to help when asked. Again, he is loyal to Stanhope, but in a less obvious, more considered manner. He is not blind to Stanhope's faults, but understands their cause and his age and experience allow him to be more tolerant of his surroundings and of the behaviour of others.

Hibbert is the "Black Sheep" of the family, and he sometimes embarrasses those around him by his comments and outbursts. He is the only selfish member of the "family", and his loyalties lie entirely with himself. He shows little or no respect for Stanhope or his fellow officers and his main concern is how to avoid any further involvement in the war.

Mason, in his role as cook, is the equivalent of the household servant, tending to the needs of the family. His loyalty is to all of them, but he answers mainly to Stanhope, who is perceived as the head of the house.

HUMOUR

There is a very effective use of humour, usually of a 'gallows' style, throughout the play.

Very early on, during Hardy's conversation with Osborne, the use of humour demonstrates the need for relief from the everyday horrors of war. The number of rats, the condition of the dugout and beds, the poor storage of ammunition, all of which are very important, are treated in a flippant, lighthearted manner. Other matters, too are treated in the same way, for example the lack of pepper to go with the officer's soup brings a wry comment from Trotter, whose interest in food provides the source of several other jokes. The fact that important and insignificant issues are treated in the same manner shows that, even things which in peacetime might seem unimportant, can, at times of extreme stress, take on a completely different emphasis.

This use of humour actually helps define the surroundings and the men's state of mind. This could probably have been achieved without the humour, but it would have been less effective, especially when one remembers that *Journey's End* is a play and is, therefore, meant to be seen as a performance. The setting of the dugout and the building tension needs some form of relief, otherwise the audience would find it too oppressive. The realistic use of humour makes the whole situation more human, which in turn draws the audience into the world of these men.

Sherriff's use of humour is, at times, more subtle - for example near the end of the play, just before the attack, when Trotter is singing in his dugout, Stanhope throws him a few coins, as though he were a street performer, and Trotter replies in kind. This humour helps in the creation of the atmosphere of camaraderie which is what has kept the men going in the dugout. This is reflected in many of the memoirs written by soldiers who served during the First World

War. Without being able to crack a joke, or have a laugh, the tension would have been almost unbearable.

COMPARISONS

Although the task of comparing one book, play or poem with another tends to be more common once a student has reached their A-levels, it is good practice for GCSE students to get into the habit of reading as widely as possible. This helps with the interpretation and understanding of literature, as well as enabling the student to have a broader perspective of the time during which a piece was written, and how this can influence the writing. The following provides a series of topics contained in *Journey's End* which could be compared or contrasted with other literature of the First World War.

MALE RELATIONSHIPS

The first important point to note, within this topic, is the time of publication. *Journey's End* was first published in 1929, which would have made an openly homosexual relationship between two characters impossible, being as homosexuality was, at that time, illegal. This also applies to other books published at that time, such as Remarque's *All Quiet on the Western Front* (1929) and Rebecca West's *The Return of the Soldier* (1918). Novels which have been published in the second half of the twentieth century such as Susan Hill's *Strange Meeting* (1971) and Sebastian Barry's *A Long Long Way* (2005) did not have this restriction and the modern authors are therefore able to be more explicit in their content and language, if they choose. However, this difference in the date of publication does not necessarily mean that the more modern authors always refer to this type of relationship.

In *Journey's End* the main relationship explored by students is usually that between Stanhope and Raleigh. Stanhope is the senior officer and Raleigh is the new recruit, determined to do well. These two men knew each other before the war and, in fact, Stanhope has "an understanding" with Raleigh's sister. They attended the same school and, Stanhope being good at sport, became an object of hero-worship to Raleigh, and probably many of the other boys at school, even before the war. This has been enhanced by his long service in the trenches, the award of an MC and his command of a Company. Raleigh's feelings for Stanhope could be said to border on a schoolboy "crush", although that is open to interpretation and his somewhat gushing descriptions of Stanhope could be put down to his youthful enthusiasm. He clearly looks up to his friend, while Stanhope feels under great pressure to protect the younger man - an almost impossible task, given their current surroundings. Stanhope's reactions to Raleigh are also tempered by his fear that Raleigh will inform his family, and therefore his sister, of the effect that the war has had on Stanhope's personality. The impression created is that Stanhope has always been popular with Raleigh's family and he is terrified of losing their respect. He has, in fact, managed to avoid seeing either his or Raleigh's family for some time - he would prefer them all to remember him how he was and he can cope better knowing that they continue to believe in him. There is no hint of homosexual love between these two men - in fact Raleigh seems to feel quite honoured that there is a budding romance between his sister and Stanhope.

Another equally important relationship in *Journey's End* is the one between Stanhope and Osborne. Here, although he is the junior officer, it is really Osborne who is portrayed as the stronger character of the two. His knowledge and understanding of Stanhope enable him to sympathise with his Commanding Officer. He still does his duty while protecting Stanhope from his own self-destruction. Sherriff's portrayal of this relationship helps to demonstrate Stanhope's comparative youth and contrasts it with the responsibilities he now has to bear. Stanhope is occasionally portrayed as almost childlike, which gives this relationship a father and son perspective. If anything, one feels that the roles should be reversed and that Osborne should be in charge - but like much else in this portrayal of the war - things are not always as they should be. Osborne unashamedly declares his love for Stanhope right at the beginning of the play, but the audience is under no misapprehension that this is a romantic love. He is stating a depth of feeling which shows how much Stanhope means to him - he would willingly follow Stanhope to Hell - but this is due to Osborne's unlimited respect for him, coupled with a mutual understanding and compassion.

A different perspective of a male relationship can be seen in Susan Hill's novel *Strange Meeting*. The two main characters in this story, Barton and Hilliard, fall deeply in love. There is no evidence that their love is necessarily physical, but that does not make it any less intense and meaningful - if anything the opposite is the case. Hilliard comes from a background devoid of affection and, finding this in Barton and his family, he is able, for the first time in his life, to experience love. There is not really an element of hero-worship between Barton and Hilliard, although the latter is slightly older and far more experienced. The portrayal of this relationship demonstrates the strength of love as an emotion: it can overcome everything - even the death of one of the parties involved and those touched by it can grow, gaining strength of character and understanding of others.

In *Strange Meeting*, the author is free to hint at a homosexual relationship, arguably leaving it open to the reader's interpretation. This was not a freedom which R C Sherriff would have been able to enjoy. It is unlikely that the play would have been performed had the content appeared homosexual. People were still keen to ensure that the love that had existed between men during the war was "the right kind of love".

The way in which the war affects these relationships varies. In *Strange Meeting*, without the war, there may not have been a relationship in the first place. Barton and Hilliard come from very different backgrounds and meet for the first time at the front. In fact, the whole of their time together is spent there. They know that they might die at any moment and this serves to intensify their feelings for one another. The sense of impending loss and danger adds to the fear and risk necessarily involved in such a close friendship between two officers at this time.

In *Journey's End*, the circumstances of the main relationship are different. Stanhope and Raleigh, had a pre-existing friendship so the entrance of the war into their lives has a profound effect on their relationship. Gone are the days of school cricket and rugby with Stanhope looking after his younger friend. Stanhope, who has been serving for many years, has become war-weary; his personality has changed, almost beyond recognition; his outlook has become tempered by his experiences. Sherriff shows us this disintegration of Stanhope's character through Raleigh's eyes, enabling us to experience his loss of innocence which occurs, in part, as he witnesses his friend's breakdown. Any trust which may have existed between these two before the war is now gone, as Stanhope realises he is no longer the same person that Raleigh used to worship. He cannot live up to Raleigh's high expectations and this only serves to heighten his sense of failure and make him more resentful of Raleigh's presence, as a reminder of the man he once was.

RESPONSIBILITY

Another aspect of the war, which is worthy of examination is that of responsibility - looking after the men. In *Journey's End* it is clear throughout that Stanhope always puts his men first. He regards himself as their father-figure, although in many cases he is much younger than them. He knows and accepts that it is his responsibility to ensure that his men are at their best, both for their own benefit and for the good of the company as a whole.

In *Strange Meeting* David Barton, like Stanhope, is quite prepared to discuss his own fears in order to ease those of his men. However, Hilliard's main concern is the welfare of Barton. That is not to say that he doesn't care about the other men in his company, but he knows that, due to his own emotional inadequacies, Barton is better suited and more able to meet their needs. He feels that, for everybody's sake, but especially his own, Barton must be kept safe, and this becomes the main focus of his attention throughout the novel.

These portrayals are quite realistic and the officer commanding a company of men was often expected to be a mother-figure, as well as a father-figure, to his men. It was his responsibility to ensure that the men were fed, washed, had somewhere to sleep, kept their equipment clean etc. In addition, he also had to provide moral support to the men and listen to their problems, trying to help solve them if possible. Given the extreme youth of most of these officers, like Stanhope, it is hardly surprising that they occasionally buckled under the weight of so many demands.

One poet who typified this attitude was E. A. Mackintosh whose love for his men is the main theme of most of his poetry. *In Memoriam* is a particularly good example of this and demonstrates how much like a father-figure he felt, as well as his sense of pride at being the officer in charge of his men, for whom he had a great respect and admiration. The story behind this moving poem is interesting. During a raid, one of Mackintosh's men, Private David Sutherland, was wounded. Mackintosh carried him for some time until it became clear that the young soldier was dead and Mackintosh was forced to leave his body behind in order to help others get back to their trenches. He actually managed to bring in two other men under heavy fire and was awarded the Military Cross for his courage. Despite this, he was overwhelmed by guilt for having left Sutherland's body in No Man's Land and this poem demonstrates his feelings of inadequacy for having, in his own mind, 'failed' this young man.

THE EFFECTS OF THE WAR

The effects of the war on the individual is a popular topic for comparisons, and represented in almost every form of literature within this genre. In *Journey's End*, the most obvious subject is Stanhope, whose personality has undergone a complete transformation. The audience only know him as the war-weary, cynical and embittered man of three year's war experience. Raleigh, on the other hand, knew him before he underwent these changes and this is how the audience gets to know of the effects of the war. The extent of the change in Stanhope's character is so great that neither man really seems to recognise the other when they first meet. This is a very simple device, employed by Sherriff, which enables the audience to understand how complete the transformation has been. Raleigh's character undergoes a change too, as he becomes more experienced. He really changes after he comes back from the raid which has cost Osborne's life. He cannot understand what has happened to him, and looks to Stanhope for reassurance, which he does not receive. This shows how, despite their former friendship, and Stanhope's generally protective nature, he is no longer able to help his friend - he is simply not capable anymore.

Sometimes authors portray the consequences of war in the form of a psychological trauma. This is the case in *The Return of the Soldier* by Rebecca West. Here, the hero, Chris Baldry has lost his memory and returned to his family home believing himself still to be twenty-one years old and in a relationship with his first-love, Margaret. His wife Kitty is, needless to say, shocked by his behaviour and the story is concerned with whether Chris should have treatment to bring him back to reality, or be allowed to remain in the, far happier, world he seems to now inhabit. The reader is not told exactly what has caused Chris's loss of memory, but it is clear from his changed appearance that his experiences of the war have taken their toll on him, both physically and emotionally. This novel not only outlines the effects of the war on the men who served in it, but also the consequences for their families and loved-ones back at home.

Not all authors use such obvious methods of demonstrating the effects of war on the individual. In many cases, it is not one single event which has the greatest impact, but a gradual wearing down of the nerves. One good example of this is *All Quiet on the Western Front*, in which Erich Maria Remarque shows how a young man, Paul Bäumer, sees all of his friends and comrades die or be badly wounded until eventually he gives up all hope for his own future. He believes that, if he survives, he may never be able to pick up the threads of his life before the war. This gradual breakdown which takes place during the novel shows how, eventually, everyone - even the most optimistic - reaches a point where they can simply not take any more.

DEATH AND LOSS

The ways in which the characters deal with death is as varied as their own personalities and depends on their relationship with the person who has died. In *Journey's End*, Osborne's death is treated differently by the two main characters. Raleigh seems to feel guilty that he has survived while Osborne has died. This is partly because he has come to understand that Osborne was an essential character in Stanhope's life and he feels that he is somehow responsible for his loss. Also, he seems to be deeply affected by what he has witnessed during the raid, he becomes much quieter and more reserved than he had been previously and all of his enthusiasm has gone. Stanhope, who has lost his best friend, reacts differently. To Raleigh, and the audience it *appears* that Stanhope does not care - he carries on as normal - even having a celebratory meal and joking around with the other officers. This is because he knows that to think about Osborne's death will stop him functioning. He must continue to perform his duties because his men are relying on him. In his nervous state, Stanhope understands that he cannot afford the luxury of grief - he would be unable to cope if he actually did dwell on Osborne's death, and would probably fall apart completely. Stanhope is not given the opportunity to dwell on Raleigh's death as he is called upon to meet his own fate, although it is interesting to note that he touches Raleigh's head just before leaving the dugout, which seems to be an act of love and tenderness which we have not witnessed in Stanhope before.

Strange Meeting is probably one of the hopeful pieces of First World War literature, yet the surviving character, Hilliard, has so many losses to contend with. Not only has his beloved Barton been killed but his own leg has been amputated. Barton's death has always been his worst fear - he has always been unsure, having discovered love and his own capacity for it, that he could carry on living without the object of that love. Due to this, he feels that the loss of his leg is of secondary importance. His own family hardly know how to react to him, but Barton's family pour out their affection and through this he is able to face the future.

Erich Maria Remarque puts his central character Paul Bäumer in *All Quiet on the Western Front*, through many harrowing experiences of loss. His friends - many of whom he was at school with - all die, until he is the only one left. For Paul, however, the most traumatic of these deaths is not one of his schoolfriends, but his comrade Stanislaus Katczinsky. Paul and Kat (as he is called) are together when Kat is injured. Paul carries his friend to a medical station where the orderly says they are too late - Kat is dead. At this moment Paul feels as if his life has ended: he can no longer feel anything but merely exists from that point onwards. Effectively, his life ceases with the loss of his friend.

Several poets wrote movingly of their grief and facing the future after so many deaths. Edith Nesbit, for example, in *The Fields of Flanders* writes of the debt of gratitude she feels for the sacrifices being demanded of, and made by so many young men. This is a debt which, in her view, can never be repaid. This sentiment is echoed in Wilfrid Wilson Gibson's *Lament* which beautifully evokes his sense of loss. Gibson is asking here how he is supposed to carry on living knowing that so many have given up everything to gain his freedom. This sense of gratitude, mixed with grief and even an element of guilt results in everything he does and sees being tinged with heartbreak - a feeling which he realises he will have to live with for the rest of his life. To Gibson, the pain of such a life is worse than death itself.

Some poets addressed poems to specific people who had died. For example Vera Brittain's poem *Perhaps* is addressed to her fiancé Roland Leighton who died on 23rd December 1915. In this poem she recites, with great sadness, all of the things she will no longer enjoy or will never be able to do, because he is not with her. Siegfried Sassoon's poem *To Any Dead Officer* was originally addressed to Lieutenant E. L. Orme who was killed in action on 27th May 1917. Here, Sassoon reminisces about happier times, when they had laughed together, before going on to describe his friend's death and how pointless it seems. Although, in typical Sassoon style, the poem ends on a note of irony, his emotions are very much on the surface in this piece and his acute sense of loss, which is thinly masked by humour, is profoundly moving. The sense that some were unable to ever forget their war experiences and the losses they suffered, is brought to life in Edmund Blunden's poem *1916 seen from 1921*. Here he describes a tremendous feeling of loss and sadness. The reader becomes acutely aware that he is biding his time, waiting for his life to return to him, so that he can once again be at peace in his beloved countryside, but one also realises that he never really achieved this aim. Like so many others, he was never truly able to forget.

ESSAY QUESTIONS AND ADVICE

The inclusion of essay questions and advice in this guide does not mean that these topics and/or themes will occur in forthcoming examination or coursework essays. The intention of this section of the study guide is to encourage students to look more thoroughly into a given theme, topic or character and then learn to apply this method to other studies.

Question One

Explain Stanhope's reaction to the arrival of Raleigh, and his continued anger towards his former schoolfriend during the course of the play.

Some points to consider:

- Think about Stanhope's immediate reaction to Raleigh - he is shocked, but also angry and disturbed, becoming thoughtful and distracted.
- As the play progresses, Stanhope becomes more angry towards Raleigh, especially following Osborne's death.
- There are many possible reasons behind Stanhope's attitude, including: his fear that Raleigh will reveal his changed nature to his family and, specifically, to Madge; the reminder which Raleigh provides of his own lost youth and innocence; and his fear at having to protect Raleigh from harm in the trenches - a near impossible task.

In answering a question like this, students need to show that they have understood the characters involved, and can interpret their actions, using relevant quotes from the text where necessary to back up these opinions.

Question Two

The character of Hibbert is very different from the other officers in the dugout. Explain these differences and your understanding of Hibbert's significance to the play.

Some points to consider:

- You have to give your interpretation of Hibbert's personality. Explain how he reacts with the others and how they behave towards him.
- Assessing *why* Hibbert is different from the others is more difficult since we are not provided with much background information, so students must form their own interpretation. For example, one of the functions of Hibbert's character could be to help demonstrate Stanhope's personality.
- Stanhope's acceptance of Hibbert's character - although he finds it loathsome himself - makes the audience question their own viewpoint. By making the audience dislike a character, such as Hibbert, it could be that Sherriff was implying that they, like Stanhope, should try to sympathise with *all* of the men, not just the nicer, more gentlemanly ones.

A question like this requires a great deal of interpretation, especially when the character is a minor one, of whom we are told little. Students need to show that they understand the role of such a character and demonstrate a knowledge of the author's possible motives in including such a personality.

Question Three

How does the author make use of humour in the play and do you consider that this is done effectively.

Some points to consider:

- How does Sherriff use humour? Where does the humour occur? This play is not intended to be a comedy, but the humour is there, nonetheless.
- Most of the humourous elements involve Hardy, Mason and Trotter. Hardy, for example, at the beginning of the play, makes many wry and comical comments to Osborne, which helps to set the scene, while also making the audience aware that the play is not going to be all doom and gloom.
- Why does Sherriff use humour? There are many reasons for this, including: to lighten the mood, preventing the audience from becoming too depressed; to help with the audience's understanding of certain characters; and finally, because it is realistic. Life in the trenches was not all depressing, and many men used humour to help them endure both the fear and the boredom.

A question like this requires a good knowledge of the piece being studied. For example, the student must not only show an understanding of where humour is being used, but also how and why, therefore requiring an interpretation of the author's intentions when he was writing the play.

GENERAL ADVICE TO STUDENTS

Although examinations can seem daunting, especially when the topic is as wide as First World War Literature, it is worth remembering the following simple tips:

- Be prepared. Read as much as possible beforehand; make sure you have revised well enough.

- Read the question. In other words, read it carefully, several times if necessary to be sure that you have a full understanding of what is expected. It is a very simple mistake to think you have understood the requirements only to find that you have completely misinterpreted them.

- Answer the question. Another common error is to get stuck in a train of thought and forget that what you are writing might not actually be answering the question in hand. You should stick to the topic required, even though you might have thought of a brilliant piece of analysis - if it doesn't relate to the question, it doesn't belong in your essay.

- Allow enough time. The examination paper will give you a guide as to how long to allow for each question. Think about the fact that you must plan your essay, deciding in advance how you want to approach the topic in hand. Don't forget to allow a few minutes at the end, just to check over what you have written.

Good luck!

FURTHER READING

To the Last Man: Spring 1918
by Lyn MacDonald

As with all of Lyn MacDonald's excellent books, To the Last Man tells its story through the words of the people who were there. It is not restricted to a British perspective, but tells of the first few months of 1918 and their momentous consequences from every angle. The author gives just the right amount of background information of a political and historical nature to keep the reader interested and informed, while leaving the centre-stage to those who really matter... the men themselves. This is an invaluable book for anyone studying Journey's End as it helps, probably more than any other book, in the understanding of the personalities involved and the time through which they were living.

Strange Meeting
by Susan Hill

Strange Meeting is a beautiful and moving book. It is the story of two young men, who meet in the worst circumstances, yet manage to overcome their surroundings and form a deep and lasting friendship. Susan Hill writes so evocatively that the reader is automatically drawn into the lives of these men: the sights, sounds and even smells which they witness are brought to life. It is a book about war and its effects; it is also a story of love, both conventional and 'forbidden'; of human relationships of every variety. This is a tale told during the worst of times, about the best of men.

Not About Heroes
by Stephen MacDonald

Probably one of the most underrated First World War plays, this details the meeting between Wilfred Owen and Siegfried Sassoon. It is a humourous, tragic and above all, moving account of this friendship and is based on diary entries and extracts from autobiographies.

The Complete Memoirs of George Sherston
by Siegfried Sassoon

An autobiographical account of Sassoon's life before and during the First World War. Sassoon has changed the names of the characters and George Sherston (Sassoon) is not a poet. This trilogy (made up of Memoirs of a Fox Hunting Man, Memoirs of an Infantry Officer and Sherston's Progress) demonstrates the effects of the war on both the serving soldiers and those left at home.

For a list of the fictional characters and their factual counterparts, see Appendix II of **Siegfried Sassoon** *by John Stuart Roberts*.

The Return of the Soldier
by Rebecca West

Written in 1918, this home-front novel gives a useful insight into the trauma of war, as seen through the eyes of three women. Chris Baldry, an officer and husband of Kitty, returns home suffering from shell-shock and amnesia, believing that he is still in a relationship with Margaret Allington - his first love. Kitty, Margaret and Chris's cousin, Jenny, must decide whether to leave Chris in his make-believe world, safe from the war; or whether to 'cure' him and risk his future welfare once he returns to being a soldier.

All Quiet on the Western Front
by Erich Maria Remarque

Written from first-hand experience of life in the trenches, this novel is the moving account of the lives of a group of young German soldiers during the First World War. The fact that this, often shocking, story is told from a German perspective demonstrates the universal horrors of the war and the sympathy between men of both sides for others enduring the same hardships as themselves.

These books and others may be purchased through our Web site bookstore at: www.greatwarliterature.co.uk/bookstore.html

In addition, students of *Journey's End* could also watch *Blackadder Goes Forth* starring Rowan Atkinson paying particular attention to the final episode. Although this screenplay was written in the late 20th century, much of the atmosphere and 'gallows' humour could prove useful in understanding this play, especially when students are unable to see a live performance.

BIBLIOGRAPHY

The First World War
by John Keegan

Chronology of the Great War, 1914-1918
Edited by Lord Edward Gleichen

To the Last Man: Spring 1918
by Lyn MacDonald

Rosebriars Trust
rosebriars.org.uk

Journey's End
by R C Sherriff

Strange Meeting
by Susan Hill

The Return of the Soldier
by Rebecca West

All Quiet on the Western Front
by Erich Maria Remarque

Scars Upon My Heart
Edited by Catherine Reilly

Never Such Innocence
Edited by Martin Stephen

The British Expeditionary Force 1914-15
Bruce Gudmundsson

OTHER GREAT WAR LITERATURE STUDY GUIDE TITLES

Great War Literature Study Guide Paperbacks:

Paperback Books

All Quiet on the Western Front	ISBN 9781905378302
Birdsong	ISBN 9781905378234
Journey's End A-Level Study Guide	ISBN 9781905378401
Regeneration	ISBN 9781905378227
Strange Meeting	ISBN 9781905378210
The Return of the Soldier	ISBN 9781905378357
Female Poets of the First World War - Vol. I	ISBN 9781905378258
War Poets of the First World War - Vol. I	ISBN 9781905378241

Great War Literature Study Guide E-Books:

Novels & Plays

All Quiet on the Western Front	ISBN 9781905378319
Birdsong	ISBN 9781905378074
Journey's End	ISBN 9781905378005
Regeneration	ISBN 9781905378067
Strange Meeting	ISBN 9781905378050
The Return of the Soldier	ISBN 9781905378364

Poets

Harold Begbie	ISBN 9781905378265
Edmund Blunden	ISBN 9781905378388
Rupert Brooke	ISBN 9781905378036
Female War Poets 1	ISBN 9781905378111
Female War Poets 2	ISBN 9781905378326
Female War Poets 3	ISBN 9781905378270

Wilfrid Wilson Gibson	ISBN 9781905378142
Julian Grenfell	ISBN 9781905378081
Ivor Gurney	ISBN 9781905378340
E A Mackintosh	ISBN 9781905378333
John McCrae	ISBN 9781905378159
Robert Nichols	ISBN 9781905378029
Wilfred Owen	ISBN 9781905378012
Jessie Pope	ISBN 9781905378104
Isaac Rosenberg	ISBN 9781905378135
Siegfried Sassoon	ISBN 9781905378043
Charles Hamilton Sorley	ISBN 9781905378098
Edward Thomas	ISBN 9781905378128
Robert Ernest Vernède	ISBN 9781905378296
Arthur Graeme West	ISBN 9781905378289

Please note that e-books are only available direct from our Web site at www.greatwarliterature.co.uk and cannot be purchased through bookshops.